THE SUN

The Star of Our Solar System

by Ellen Lawrence

Consultants:

Suzy Gazlay, MA
Recipient, Presidential Award for Excellence in Science Teaching

Kevin Yates
Fellow of the Royal Astronomical Society

Published in 2014 by Ruby Tuesday Books Ltd.

Editor: Mark J. Sachner
Designer: Emma Randall

Photo Credits:
NASA: Cover, 4–5, 6, 9 (bottom), 13, 14–15, 18–19;
Ruby Tuesday Books: 7, 22; Shutterstock: 8–9, 10–11,
12, 16–17, 20; Science Photo Library: 21.

Library of Congress Control Number: 2013939983

ISBN 978-1-909673-00-7

Printed and published in the United States of America

For further information including rights and
permissions requests, please contact our Customer
Service Department at 877-337-8577.

Contents

Words shown in **bold** in the text are explained in the glossary.

Meet the Sun

Millions of miles from Earth, a giant, burning ball of light shines in the blackness of space.

Here on Earth, we see its light and feel its heat.

Without its light and heat, our world would be dark and freezing cold.

No life on our home **planet** could survive.

The huge, shining ball is the Sun, and it makes life on Earth possible!

You should never look directly at the Sun because it will badly damage your eyes. Scientists take photos of the Sun, like the ones in this book, using special equipment. Then everyone can safely look at the amazing photos.

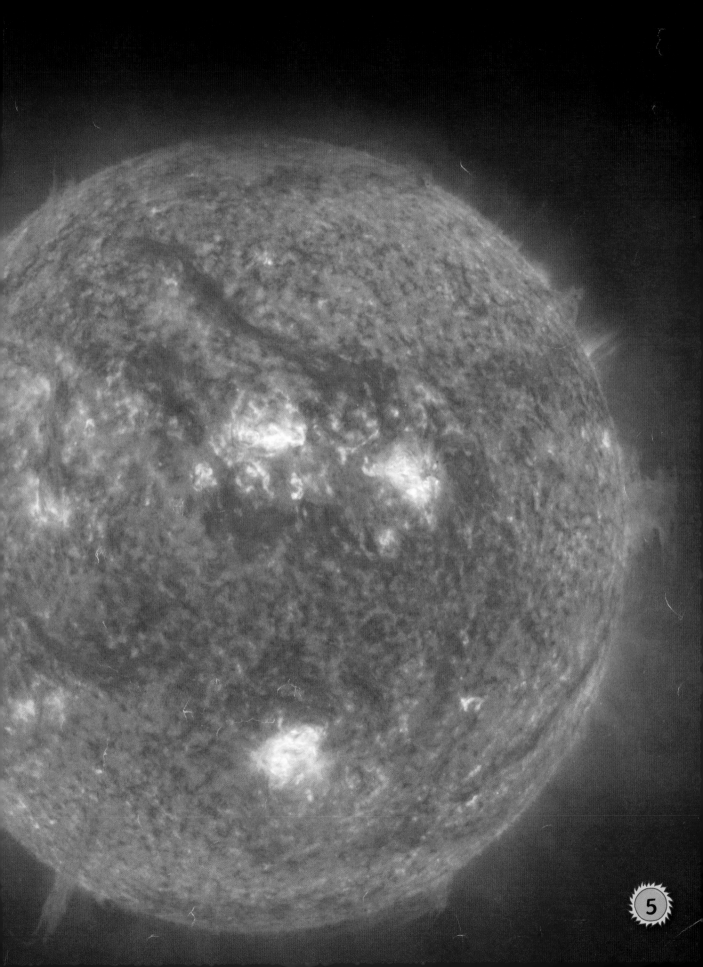

5

The Solar System

The Sun is at the center of a large family of space objects.

All these objects are **orbiting**, or circling, around the Sun.

There are eight planets orbiting the Sun.

The planets are called Mercury, Venus, our home planet Earth, Mars, Jupiter, Saturn, Uranus, and Neptune.

Icy **comets** and rocky **asteroids** are also circling around the Sun.

Together, the Sun, the planets, and other space objects are called the **solar system**.

Asteroids are huge space rocks. Most of the asteroids orbiting the Sun are in a ring called the asteroid belt.

An asteroid

The Solar System
The Sun is at the center of the solar system.

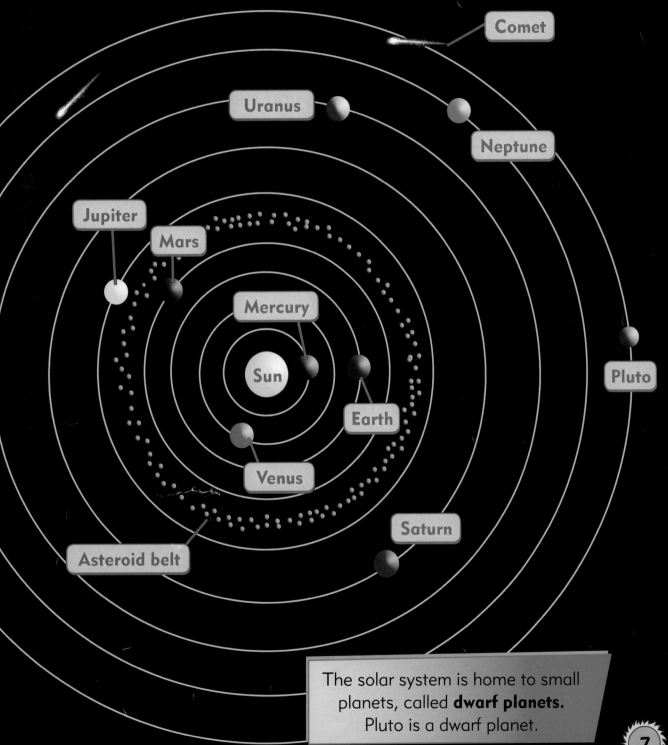

Comet

Uranus

Neptune

Jupiter

Mars

Mercury

Sun

Pluto

Earth

Venus

Saturn

Asteroid belt

The solar system is home to small planets, called **dwarf planets.** Pluto is a dwarf planet.

What Is the Sun?

When you look at the night sky, you see hundreds and hundreds of **stars**.

Our Sun is also a star, just like all those others!

The Sun looks huge in the sky compared to other stars because we are close to it.

All the other stars in the sky are much farther from Earth than the Sun.

Like all stars, the Sun is a giant ball of burning **gases**.

As the gases burn, they create light and heat.

Earth is 93 million miles (150 million km) from the Sun. The Sun is so huge, however, that from Earth it still looks big in the sky.

The Sun

The Sun

Surface of Pluto

This picture shows how it might look
to stand on Pluto. Pluto is much
farther from the Sun than Earth.
From Pluto, the Sun would look like
a bright star shining in the sky.

Day and Night

During the day, we see the Sun in the sky, but at night it disappears.

This happens because our Earth is **rotating**, or spinning, like a top.

As Earth rotates, different parts of our planet have day and night.

When the place where you live faces toward the Sun, it is daytime for you.

As it spins away from the Sun's light, darkness falls and it is night.

The Sun

Day

Night

Earth

This picture shows how day and night look on Earth. It's daytime on the half of the planet that's facing the Sun. On the other half, it's nighttime. In real life, the Sun and Earth are not this close.

A Closer Look at the Sun

The Sun and all the other objects in the solar system are moving through space.

As it travels through space, the Sun is also rotating, just as Earth does.

It takes Earth 24 hours, or one Earth day, to rotate once.

The giant Sun takes about 25 Earth days to spin around once.

Compared to Earth, the Sun is enormous.

It would be possible to fit 1 million Earths inside the Sun!

This picture shows how the Sun rotates.

Sun

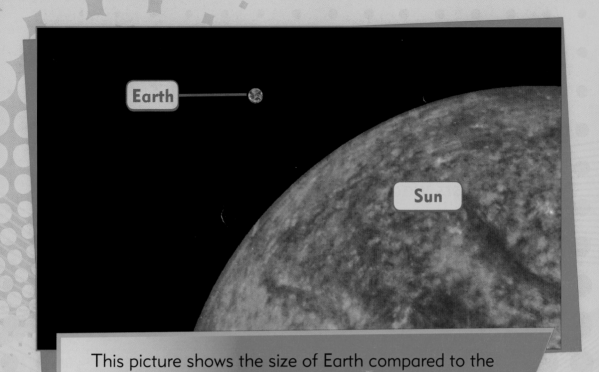

This picture shows the size of Earth compared to the Sun. Only a small part of the Sun can fit into the picture.

The Sun

The supergiant star Antares

Some stars are much bigger than our Sun. This picture shows the size of the Sun compared to a supergiant star called Antares (an-TAHR-eez). Now the Sun looks tiny!

Our Amazing Star

As scientists watch the Sun using special equipment, they see many amazing things.

Sometimes it looks as if there has been an explosion on the Sun.

These sudden bright flashes are called solar flares.

Sometimes giant loops of super-hot gas erupt from the Sun.

These glowing loops can stretch into space for hundreds of thousands of miles.

Solar flare

This is a photo of a solar flare.

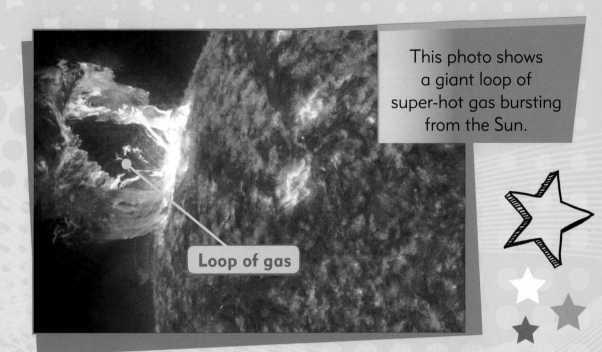

This photo shows
a giant loop of
super-hot gas bursting
from the Sun.

Loop of gas

Sunspot

This photo shows dark sunspots on the Sun.
A sunspot is a place that's cooler than the rest
of the Sun's surface. The largest sunspot in this
photo is bigger than Earth.

Where Did the Sun Go?

As Earth orbits the Sun, the Moon is orbiting Earth.

Sometimes, the Sun, Earth, and Moon are in just the right position to make something exciting happen.

We see the Moon pass between Earth and the Sun.

As the Moon passes across the face of the Sun, it blocks the Sun's light.

This is called an **eclipse**.

The sky may even get darker during an eclipse.

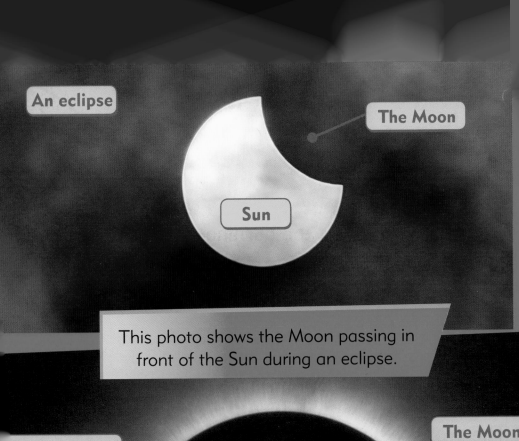

An eclipse

The Moon

Sun

This photo shows the Moon passing in front of the Sun during an eclipse.

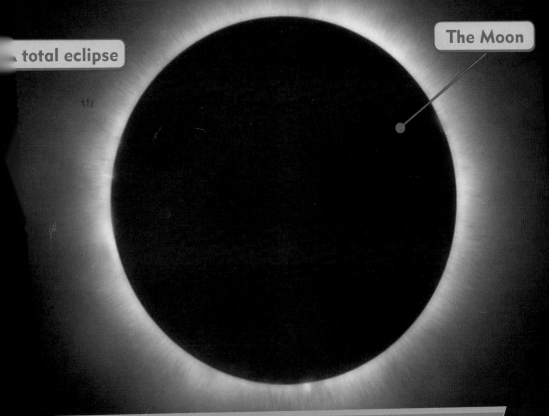

total eclipse

The Moon

Sometimes the Moon completely blocks the Sun. This is called a total eclipse. During a total eclipse, day seems to turn into night for just a few minutes.

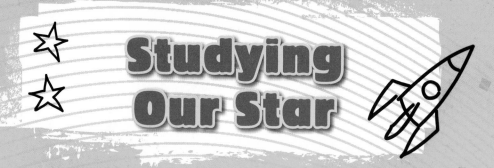

Studying Our Star

Humans cannot visit the burning-hot Sun, but we can study it using space **probes**.

A space probe known as SDO is studying the Sun right now.

SDO is orbiting Earth about 22,000 miles (36,000 km) above Earth's surface.

The probe beams a photo of the Sun back to Earth every second.

We couldn't survive on Earth without our Sun.

So it's important that we learn everything we can about our very special star.

SDO probe

Scientist

This photo shows scientists working on SDO before its mission began.

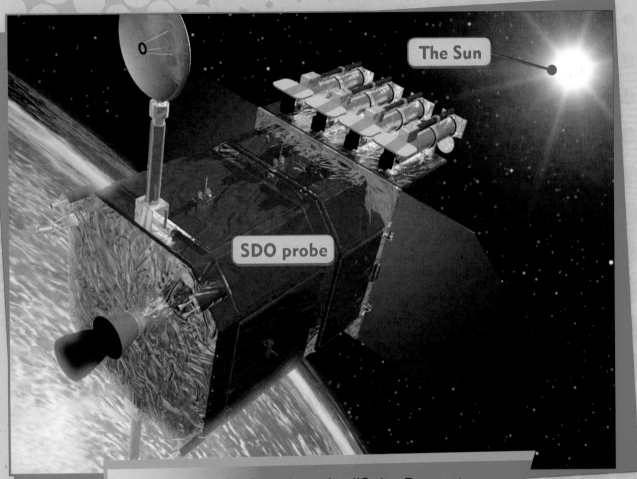

The Sun

SDO probe

The name SDO is short for "Solar Dynamics Observatory." This picture shows how SDO might look as it flies above Earth.

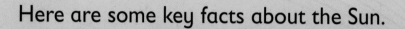

The Sun Fact File

Here are some key facts about the Sun.

How the Sun got its name

The Romans called the Sun "Sol." In English, the word "Sol" means "Sun."

The Sun's size

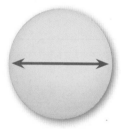

864,337 miles (1,391,016 km) across

How long it takes for the Sun to rotate once

About 25 Earth days

The Sun's speed

The Sun is traveling through space at about 490,000 miles per hour (790,000 km/h).

Temperature on the Sun

The temperature on the Sun's surface is 9,900°F (5,500°C)

The Sun's distance from Earth

The closest Earth gets to the Sun is 91,402,640 miles (147,098,291 km).

The farthest Earth gets from the Sun is 94,509,460 miles (152,098,233 km)

Solar system sizes

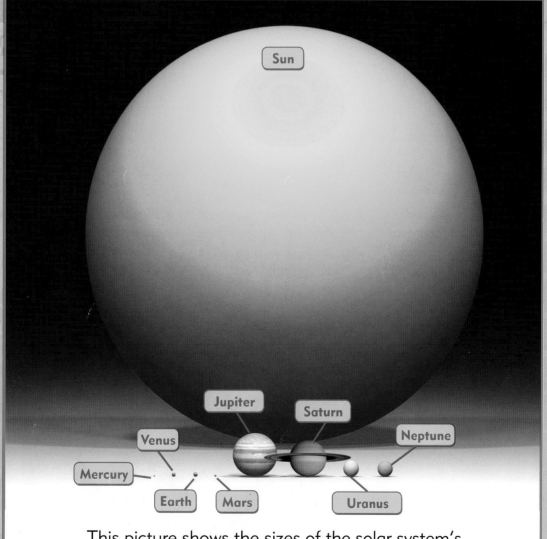

This picture shows the sizes of the solar system's planets compared to the Sun and each other.

Get Crafty
Melted Wax Crayon Sun

Using melted wax crayons, make a colorful sun catcher.

You will need:

- Wax paper
- Scissors
- Yellow, red, and orange wax crayons
- A cheese grater
- An iron and an adult helper to use the iron

1. Cut two circles from the wax paper that are about the size of dinner plates.

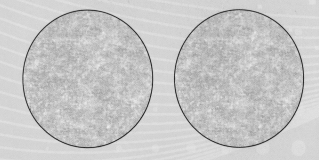

2. Grate the crayons onto one circle of wax paper. Be very careful not to rub your fingers against the grater.

3. Place the other piece of wax paper on top of the grated crayons to make a crayon sandwich.

4. Now ask an adult to iron your crayon sandwich using a cool iron. Keep ironing until the crayons melt and swirl together.

5. Hang your melted crayon Sun in a window to catch the Sun's light, or use it to make a space picture.

Glossary

asteroid (AS-teh-royd) A large rock that is orbiting the Sun. An asteroid can be as small as a car or bigger than a mountain.

comet (KAH-mit) A space object made of ice, rock, and dust that is orbiting the Sun.

dwarf planet (DWARF PLAN-et) A round object in space that is orbiting the Sun. Dwarf planets are much smaller than the eight main planets.

eclipse (ee-KLIPSS) The blocking of the light from one space object by another. During a solar eclipse, the Sun's light is blocked by the Moon.

gas (GASS) A substance, such as oxygen or helium, that does not have a definite shape or size.

orbit (OR-bit) To circle, or move around, another object.

planet (PLAN-et) A large object in space that is orbiting the Sun. Some planets, such as Earth, are made of rock. Others, such as Jupiter, are made of gases and liquids.

probe (PROBE) A spacecraft that does not have any people aboard. Probes are usually sent to planets or other objects in space to take photographs and collect information. They are controlled by scientists on Earth.

rotate (ROH-tate) To spin around.

solar system (SOH-ler SIS-tem) The Sun and all the objects that orbit it, such as planets, their moons, asteroids, and comets.

star (STAR) A huge ball of burning gases in space. Our Sun is a star.

Index

Read More

Hughes, Catherine D.
*First Big Book of Space
(National Geographic Little
Kids)*. Washington, D.C.:
The National Geographic
Society (2012).

Oxlade, Chris. *Space
Watch: The Sun (Eye
on Space)*. New York:
PowerKids Press (2010).

Learn More Online

To learn more about the Sun, go to
www.rubytuesdaybooks.com/sun